About (the) Illustrator

Name: ....

Age: .... Hometown: ....

One of the bravest things I ever did was:

....

....

Something I like to do outside is:

....

....

If I were a fairy, my favorite thing to do would be:

....

....

Flora Fairy's Big Ideas

COMPENDIUM®

kids™

inspiring possibilities.™

Flora is a tiny fairy.

She sleeps inside a flower.

She is very strong. Flora helps a baby bird who has

fallen

out

of

his

nest.

And Flora is brave.
She leaps across the leaves
floating on the pond.

She jumps from a tree branch using a feather as a parachute.

She rides on her best friend,
a bumble bee.

They eat honey with wild berries and drink dew together.

Flora likes to give people good ideas.

She stands on their shoulders and *whispers* in their ears.

She sees a little girl on the playground who will not share her jump rope.

Flora whispers
something to her.

Then, she sprinkles some magic kindness dust.

Soon, everyone is jumping rope together!

Flora and her bumble bee
ride away.

They have lots of
other people to help.

WITH SPECIAL THANKS TO THE
ENTIRE COMPENDIUM FAMILY.

CREDITS:

Written by: M.H. Clark
Designed by: Julie Flahiff
Edited by: Amelia Riedler

ISBN: 978-1-938298-19-6

1st printing. Printed in China with soy inks. A011310001

COMPENDIUM®

kids

inspiring possibilities.™